NLP for Young Drivers

Judy Bartkowiak

Paperback ISBN 978-1-907685-37-7

ePub ISBN 978-1-907685-38-4

Mobipocket/Kindle ISBN 978-1-907685-39-1

Published in the UK by MX Publishing

335 Princess Park Manor, Royal Drive, London, N11 3GX

www.mxpublishing.co.uk

Cover design by

www.staunch.com

FOREWORD

So you've passed your driving test

Congratulations!

Your life will change. You will feel free to go out wherever you want, when you want and with whom you want. As a young person, passing your driving test probably makes more impact on your day to day life than passing a school or Uni exam so no wonder you're pleased with yourself and excited about how your life will change.

Driving represents freedom doesn't it? Freedom from having to ask for lifts, freedom from using public transport and being restricted by when and where you can go and freedom to play your own music as you drive, at the volume you want.

In fact I believe it is more fundamental than this. Driving a car is an expression of how we drive our life, understanding how one impacts the other could literally be the difference between life and death.

You can tell a great deal about someone by the way they drive, can't you? What do you want your driving to say about you?

Learning advanced driving skills is not just about improving your driving; it is about learning skills that you can apply to your whole life - for confidence, controlling your state and improving your ability to focus and achieve your goals.

This is essentially a practical book in which you are invited to make notes and get involved in the exercises.

Special thanks go to Don Palmer whose website and Driver's Handbook I highly recommend http://www.donpalmer.co.uk/

I also recommend Sir John Whitmore's book 'Superdriver'. If you are interested to read more about NLP, his book Coaching for Performance is a 'must read'.

I am an NLP Master Practitioner and Trainer based in the UK and available via Skype for consultations. You can get in touch with me via my website at http://www.engagingnlp.com where you can also buy my other NLP books including NLP for Teens.

CONTENTS

Page

INTRODUCTION

Anyone willing to improve their driving skills deserves respect. Even Formula 1 racing drivers continue to train throughout their career and never claim they are the best they can ever be, despite having won trophies.

The changes you make in your driving will also affect the rest of your life in all sorts of areas; your studies at school or college, your working life, the sports you play, your social life and your relationships with others and so on.

This is because:

- Becoming a more accomplished and confident driver will increase your self-esteem.

- By developing a more energy-efficient driving style this will leave you with more energy to enjoy other activities.

- Eliminating stress and aggression from your relationships on the road will have beneficial results in your other relationships.

- Improving your judgement and anticipation will improve your performance in sports.

Passing your driving test is just the beginning of a long and enjoyable relationship with your car and improving a life skill, in the same way you would expect to improve other skills you have such as using a computer, your sexual performance, social skills and so on.

CHAPTER 1

BASIC NLP PRINCIPLES APPLIED TO DRIVING

NLP has a number of ground rules or principles that form the basis for all the practical tools and techniques you will learn in this book.

1) Mind and Body are one

"To drive well, it is essential to synchronise mind and body to a very high degree and to process all the information gathered by the senses to produce physical actions"

Jackie Stewart wrote this in the foreword to Superdriver by Sir John Whitmore. He was ranked 5th of the world's Formula One drivers in 2009.

So let's get active right away. I want to show you how you can control your body using just your mind because the only thing preventing you from being an excellent driver is yourself.

It may be easier if you ask a friend to read out the instructions while you do the exercise.

A)

1) Stand and put your right arm straight out in front of you with your finger pointing.

2) Remain facing forwards and move your arm as far around to the side and if you can behind you, keeping your arm straight. Notice the point you reach with your finger. What are you pointing at?

3) Now close your eyes and repeat the exercise and this time visualise (imagine) going further round, staying relaxed and comfortable.

4) Now imagine getting another few inches further, again stay relaxed and comfortable.

5) And another few inches again staying relaxed and comfortable.

6) Now another few inches.

7) Open your eyes and see how much further you have managed to reach when you use the power of your mind.

B)

1) Put out your right arm, palm down

2) Your friend rests his hand lightly on your arm. He doesn't need to push on it, just enough pressure to give you something to push against.

3) Test it by pushing your arm up and notice the effort it takes.

4) Now think of something that hasn't gone well for you recently. Think about it as if it's happening now. Then raise your arm and notice how much harder it is to push your friend's hand up.

5) Break state for a moment by shaking your arm and then return to holding it out again with your friend's hand on it as before.

6) Now think of something that's gone really well recently and think of it as if it's happening now. Then raise your arm again and notice how much easier it is to push your friend's hand up.

Maybe you've been distracted by your friends in the car with you? Perhaps you've slept overnight on your mate's floor after a party and are driving back tired and somewhat hung-over? Your attention is drawn to a rather fit student coming out of college as you pull out of your parking space. You're late for class and the lights are against you all the way.

Whatever the situation there's always an excuse, someone else to blame but the culprit is a bit closer to home than that. The culprit is the gremlin inside your head, your ego that does not want to look a fool and is always right.

Sometimes your ego is asleep and you drive effortlessly, the car feels more responsive than usual, the traffic is flowing and you exchange 'thank you' waves with other drivers as you let them in and someone else does the same for you. All is right with the world and you even arrive early!

We have all experienced those two very different types of journey or states. We tend not to take any responsibility for them though. Instead we blame circumstances or 'other people'.

In this book you will learn more about how to control your state. For now, here's something to try when you are next driving.

EXPERIMENT

A sensitive touch on the steering wheel is crucial. To develop a better sense of touch put your fingertips together as if you're praying.

Relax and let the fingers touch each other lightly on the surface.

Now move them apart slightly and notice the feeling on the pads of your fingertips.

Do this when you are driving. Just rest your hands like that, lightly on the wheel, being aware of your pads.

Steering wheel sensitivity is key.

Being relaxed is the best state for driving. You can completely transform your driving when you drive like this and the car feels relaxed and smooth.

Note down here what you experienced when you drove like this.

2) *If you always do what you've always done*

then you will always get what you've always got

This is about the challenge to change. But from what to what?

Let's start with a Personal Reality Check. This is from Sir John Whitmore's book 'Superdriver'. For each question, please write your number in the box.

1. How many parking tickets have you had?

2. How many driving offences have you had?

3. How would you describe your driving on a scale of 1-10 on these factors?

1..10

Confident......................................Nervous

[ ]

Smooth...Jerky

[ ]

Relaxed..Uptight

[ ]

Skilful...Poor

[ ]

Fast...Slow

[ ]

Safe..Dangerous

[ ]

Patient......................................Impatient

[ ]

17

4. Which of the following apply to you?

a) Do you break speed limits?

       Hardly ever ☐

       All the time ☐

b) Are you ever late?

       Never ☐

       Usually ☐

c) If you know you will be late do you...

       Drive like an idiot ☐

       Drive normally ☐

d) If another driver makes a sign at you for an error you've made, do you...

       Apologise ☐

       Get angry ☐

e) When you make a mistake do you....

       Signal an apology ☐

       Attack in defence ☐

f) On a multi-lane motorway do you overtake on the inside lane?

Hardly ever ☐

All the time ☐

g) Do you know approximately how an engine, gearbox, clutch and suspension work?

Yes ☐

No ☐

5. Which three conditions worry you most:

Ice ☐

Fog ☐

Driving at night ☐

Rain ☐

Mountain roads ☐

City traffic ☐

Driving abroad ☐

Driving an unfamiliar car ☐

6. How often do you drink and drive?

   Hardly ever ☐

   A bit too often ☐

7. How often do you use your mobile/cell phone while you're driving?

   Hardly ever ☐

   A bit too often ☐

8. Are you willing to invest some time in improving your driving?

   Yes ☐

   No ☐

Has this raised your awareness of your starting point?

If the result is not what you want then you must change your own behaviour in order to get a different result.

As drivers we tend to think that it is other people who must change and we shout at them and get cross.

So here is a new way of thinking.

Do something different.

If you do something different you will get a different result.

The first way to do this is to decide what result you want. Maybe you want to stay calm and in control of your car rather than getting impatient and annoyed at tailgaters, drivers that cut you up, those who drive too slowly or don't indicate, go through red lights…………the list goes on doesn't it?!

Think of a situation that occurs frequently in your driving that you'd like to change. Write it down here.

I want to change………..

Now think about what you would like to happen. What is your desirable outcome? Write that down now. What I want to happen is.........

When you decide on what result you want, you need to be quite specific and get to the detail. What exactly do you want, from whom, when and in what way? Write this down here.

I want ....

The more specific you can be about what you want to happen; the easier it will be to decide how to change what you are currently doing in order to achieve it.

Your current behaviour pattern is dictated by your beliefs. A belief is something you hold to be true about yourself, other people on the road, pedestrians, cyclists and other road users.

Your beliefs about driving stem from your own childhood and how you were brought up, what you consider to be of value and important about how you drive your car and how others should drive. This may also have come from the mores of the culture you are from, the area or region where you live and who you spend time with in your environment as well as how your parents and friends drive.

If what you are doing is not working then look at the underlying belief for this behaviour.

Are you sure your underlying belief is sound?
Could you be carrying forward into the present
a belief that belongs in the past?

Look back at the quiz and list all the beliefs that
underpin your behaviour and write them down
here.

I believe that my driving is…………..…………

I believe that other people's driving is…………

I believe that pedestrians are …………..

I believe that cyclists are ……………

Where have those beliefs come from?

Are they valid for you today? Are they serving
you well or do they result in driving that you are
not proud of?

Could you re-think a belief so that you could make other choices of behaviour?

Whenever you find yourself thinking 'I should ....' - change it to, 'I could ......' so that you give yourself permission to do something different.

If your beliefs limit your choices of driving behaviour; increase your options and change your behaviour to get the result you want.

3) You have the resources to do whatever you want to do

There are only two causes of accidents on the road – human failure and mechanical failure. Mechanical failure accounts for less than 5% of the total. Although you cannot control other drivers' reactions, you can control your own.

Here are some of the possible internal reactions you may have experienced – impatience, arrogance, lack of concentration, lack of confidence, boredom and fear. These are the internal obstacles that prevent you being the safe, relaxed and confident driver you'd like to be.

You have a huge resource of skills and each one, when applied in different contexts gives you yet more skills and options.

When you first start driving it's easy to forget that although you haven't driven a real car before you have done lots of other things rather like it and have those skills that you can apply to this new challenge.

You have almost certainly used some sort of simulator in a games arcade, a video game or phone app. This will have exercised your hand / eye co-ordination.

So if you are feeling a low sense of self belief like that, imagine that someone else is watching you over the course of the day. What would they observe? What would they see you do?

What you do automatically or unconsciously is
a skill that someone else would observe and
admire. Pretend you are someone who doesn't
know you, observing all you do.

- Look at each thing you do over the
  course of the day and write down the
  skill you use to do that thing. Make a list
  here.

- What do you believe about doing this thing? How important is the way you do it? How well do you feel you do this thing?

The reason I do...............................

well is because I believe.......

The reason I do...............................

well is because I believe.......

The reason I do...............................

well is because I believe.......

Now list each thing you do well and give each one a score out of 10 for how important it is to you to do this thing well.

1.

2.

3.

4.

5.

- Now look at each thing you do well and ask yourself, 'What does that also mean I can do in the context of my driving?'

Write that down in a list here. You may be surprised at how you can use a skill from another part of your life in your driving.

- Whenever you are driving

  - identify the skill you need

  - think about when and where you had that skill

  - ask yourself, what was the belief you had that enabled you to use that skill

  - take on that belief now in order to access the skill.

Note that when we talk about taking on a belief in NLP we mean that we change our belief.

A belief is not a value. A value is a code you live by and that is not likely to change as it is instilled in you as a child and is governed by both your upbringing and your environment.

A belief is something you hold about the things you do and changes as you experience new situations and people. For example, you certainly hold different beliefs now from those you held as a child such as believing in Father Christmas or the Tooth Fairy!

Our beliefs about driving will have changed as a result of becoming a more experienced driver and continue to change as we experience new conditions.

Think about how you felt about your driving when you first learnt to drive, then just before you passed your test, and now, how do you feel about your driving? It's changed hasn't it? You have different beliefs about your driving now. And you have all the resources you need to become even better.

4) *If someone else can do it you can too*

This is a very empowering belief to take on board as a driver, isn't it? Do you watch Top Gear and imagine you are The Stig? Do you watch the motor racing on TV and imagine yourself in the driving seat of the winning car? How often do we see other drivers do things that we admire and would like to do ourselves?

If you have noticed a skill in someone else, the chances are that in some way you too have this skill because that is how you come to have noticed it in the first place. We say 'if you spot it, you've got it!'

You can acquire these new skills and hone existing ones by modelling (or copying) it in someone who demonstrates that skill with excellence.

How do we do it?

a) First we need to identify the skill we want.

We do this by observation. Think of someone you really rate as a driver. Observe and be intently curious about what you see and how your model (the person you want the skill from) behaves.

Watch every part of the skill, the non-verbal cues such as body language and the verbal ones, the tone of voice, language patterns, volume and pace.

Identify which part of the skill you need because it is unlikely you need all of it.

Decide which bit you need and break it into small parts that you can practice.

b) Think about the belief your model would have in order to use that skill.

Do this by reflecting 'If I did that I would be thinking I was ....'. Perhaps your model sounds confident or calm, controlled or firm?

Where in your life do you have that belief? Maybe you have that belief when you are at work, studying, with your friends or at the gym or on the sports field?

Think hard about where you have the belief and visualise yourself in that situation where the belief is strong. So dust off that skill and belief so that you have them now in your driving.

c) Now practice the precise skill you have identified.

Notice what results you get and keep practising until you get your desirable outcome.

You may find that you need more models of that skill so you can observe different

34

executions of it and talk to the models about how they do it and what they believe about the way they do it. It often takes a few different models of a skill to help you acquire it for yourself and use in a way that works for you.

Once you have mastered this modelling exercise you can use it for other areas in your life such as your studies, getting a job or your sport.

Use modelling skills as part of your ongoing personal development.

5) *There is no failure only feedback*

As we go through life, we often feel we have failed don't we? Things don't always go as well as we'd like and when we get poor marks or perform badly in sport, we feel disappointed in ourselves.

However, imagine you held a belief that there is no failure only feedback, how much more reassuring is that?

How other people respond to us is feedback. The feedback can be verbal or non verbal and we can use it to learn more about what and how we are communicating.

If we drive without consideration of others on the road we may get feedback in the form of a loud horn blown at us or rude signs with hands or the middle finger. Sometimes another driver will wind down the window and shout at us.

When you are learning, this can be annoying, after all, we all make mistakes in the first few years of driving don't we?

Learning from these mistakes is very important because this is how we become a better driver, equipped to cope with a wider range of driving situations. .

There is no <u>one</u> correct or definitive response.

When someone responds negatively to you when you're driving, they are giving you feedback that you can choose to accept or not, depending on whether it seems reasonable when set against your beliefs and values.

Their feedback is not a fact of life but simply their opinion at that moment and this will be influenced by their own internal state or mood and yours, of course.

You may be getting negative feedback because someone is just in a bad mood, feeling rough, depressed, or cross about something unrelated that has happened to them.

You have two choices when you get negative feedback. You can choose to accept it or reject it.

Accept it if you think they may have a fair point and take the opportunity to do something differently. By doing this you are using the feedback as an adult learning experience that will enable you to drive better next time.

However difficult it might be at the time, if you believe they are being reasonable in their feedback, acknowledge it with a hand wave by way of apology and learn from it.

If however, you decide that their action is unreasonable then it's best to ignore it rather than risk an accident. We will learn about anchoring later in the book and this is an excellent technique for becoming calm and relaxed as a driver.

Watch out for these types of assumptions about other drivers:

a) Generalisations

These are when we say things like 'cyclists always go through the red lights' or 'old people always drive slowly', 'women drivers!' and so on.

Generalisations are rarely true. They tend to catch us out and lead us to make a false reading of a driving situation.

For example, it is a general rule that you don't overtake on the inside - yet people do occasionally. Before moving lane on the motorway, check that someone isn't overtaking you on the inside.

Generalisations are assumptions and in a driving context are safer to check out because if you a wrong, it could be a difference between life and death on a busy motorway.

b) Deletions

When we delete the context of a situation it isn't very helpful either. An example might be when you tell yourself 'I must concentrate more on the motorway'. More than what? Be aware of what you need to focus on specifically. Is it keeping a certain distance from the car in front? Is it, making sure you don't go over the speed limit?

c) Distortions

Sometimes we make assumptions about what other drivers are making us feel. For example 'that driver in front is making me late' or 'that driver behind is making me angry'. We can't know this. We are not mind readers so we are in effect distorting the facts.

What is really happening is that we are choosing to be cross or annoyed so we need to control our own state rather than blame it on other drivers.

6) If you try, you won't succeed

How many times a day do we assure people that we will 'try' and do something? Why do we use that word 'try'?

It's because we know deep down that we may not actually have the time or inclination to do it.

Perhaps we think we don't have the skill? We want to hedge our bets really, don't we? We don't want to give a promise that we may not be able to keep and we don't want to let people down.

We also don't want to say 'no' possibly because that would appear confrontational or provoke further discussion which we don't have the time or desire to pursue. So off we go to 'try' and do that thing, knowing that we don't have to do it, we just have to 'try' to do it.

What does 'trying to do it' look like? Well it looks like someone accepting that they can't and won't do it fairly shortly after they've said they'll 'try'.

Do you 'try to drive within the speed limit' or 'try to stay awake' when driving at night? There is built-in failure in the word 'try'. Notice when you use this word and reword your sentence without the word 'try' so you are more motivated. 'Try' presupposes you will find it difficult so you are expecting to give up on the task more quickly than if your expectation was that you can do it.

There is built-in failure in the word 'try'.

Just 'do it'.

7) *The map is not the territory*

What this means is that how you see the road ahead is different from how others see it. We all have different perceptions of our driving environment depending on where we are physically, our driving experience, whether we are in a rush, feeling tired and stressed and our belief in our driving ability.

To assume our perceptions are the only correct ones would be unecological in NLP terms.

CHAPTER 2
<u>BUILDING RAPPORT WITH YOUR CAR</u>

Rapport is that sense of being at one with your car where the driving is fluid because you are communicating clearly between you. You feel relaxed and at ease.

You are aware of your car <u>visually</u> in the sense of watching the instrument panel, the road conditions, and other drivers. You are aware of what you <u>hear,</u> how the tyres sound on the road, how the engine sounds. Kinaesthetically you are aware of how the car is handling, the feel of the clutch and gears and the feel of the brakes. At every level, visual, auditory and

44

kinaesthetically you need to be in rapport with the car.

Here is an exercise you can do to increase your rapport by becoming more aware of your driving.

EXERCISE

First while you are reading this book be aware of how you are sitting, the contact point of your bottom on the chair and your back against the back of the chair. How hard is the pressure at each point? What happens if you move slightly? Do the same for the contact with your feet on the ground and for your hands on this book. As you move a little, notice how the pressure changes.

Now let's do the same thing as you drive. Focus on the pressure points between you and the seat, your hands and the wheel, your feet and the pedals. Notice the sensations and feel how they change as you drive.

Let's go inside our body now and become aware of your muscles. How tight are they? Where exactly do you feel any discomfort and what sort of feeling is it? When do you feel it? On a scale of 1-10 how strong is the sensation and does it get higher in traffic?

You might find that as you focus on the muscle and consciously relax it and maybe change your position slightly, the score will decrease.

Do this awareness test from time to time when you are driving and it will help you to both relax and be in rapport with the car.

WHAT KIND OF DRIVER ARE YOU?

There are three internal preferences – visual, auditory and kinaesthetic. These apply to you and your driving. They signify whether you are aware of what you see, what you hear or what you feel. We use all three at various times but there will be one that you prefer. Which is it?

Here's a quiz to help you find out. Tick the answer a, b or c that most often applies to you.

Q1. When you are driving do you mostly notice?

    a) What you see on the road ahead

    b) How the engine sounds

    c) How the car handles

Q2. When you look at your car do you notice?

    a) It's appearance

    b) What people say about it

    c) How you feel about it

Q3. What is most important to you about driving?

    a) Being seen in a great looking car

    b) The roar of the engine

    c) The feeling of freedom

Q4. Thinking about the interior of the car what is most important to you?

    a) What it looks like

    b) The sound system

    c) The feel of the upholstery

Q5. If you get lost do you

    a) Look at a map

    b) Ask someone for directions

    c) Go by gut instinct

If you've mostly answered 'a' then you are visual and you think in pictures and images, using expressions like 'do you see what I mean' or 'look at it from my point of view'.

The appearance of your car and you as a driver will be important to you. You will want to keep it clean and looking good. Maybe you have bought extras that enhance its appearance.

If you've mostly answered 'b' then you are auditory. You are auditory if you enjoy music, notice the sounds around you and prefer your friends to call rather than text or email. You tend to remember what people say to you or what you've heard better than what you've read.

You might use expressions like 'did you hear what I said?' or 'please be quiet'.

Choosing your sound system will be very important and you'll probably enjoy just sitting in the car listening to it even when you aren't driving.

You'll notice the engine and exhaust noises and choose a car you like the sound of. Maybe you will have extras like a sub woofer and back box.

If you've mostly answered 'c' then you are kinaesthetic and quite an active person and enjoy being on the go. Exercise and fitness is important to you and you like to have physical contact with your friends and your family.

You notice the temperature and feel uncomfortable if it's not right.

You may use expressions like 'let's get going' or 'that doesn't feel right' because you are very sensitive to atmosphere.

You will have chosen a car that feels right to you and you like the way it handles and feels when you're driving it. The way the gears engage and the actual driving mechanism, the clutch and breaking system will also be important to you.

Having established whether you are a visual, auditory or kinaesthetic driver let's now work out which meta programmes you use.

These are different ways of processing the information you receive and how you approach driving and other activities you do.

The first is big chunk/small chunk.

You are big chunk if you set off on a drive vaguely knowing where you're going and having a rough idea how long it will take, knowing roughly how many miles you do to the gallon and how much petrol your car takes.

A small chunk driver knows exactly all this information and has an interest in detail. If you are small chunk you know your car very well and would be unlikely to run out of petrol or let it run low on oil. You attend to the detail of driving and running a car.

Another is towards/away from

A driver who is 'towards' thinks about what they want from a car and from the driving experience. An 'away from' driver talks about what they don't want for example 'I don't want a car that will drink lots of petrol', 'I don't want a car that will be expensive to fix'.

Choices/Process is about your preference for choices or whether you just prefer to make a decision and get on with things.

A choices driver would consider their choice of car extensively comparing models, value for money, reliability and whatever other factor was important. A process driver would just make a list of what was important and then buy one so that the task is achieved and they can get on with the next one.

Internal/external referencing

Someone who is internally referenced would buy whatever car they wanted, within budget of course and would only care what they thought without reference to other people's views.

An externally referenced driver would ask all their mates what car they liked and what they thought of each of the options they were considering. They would read reviews and be swayed by the people they considered to have a valid opinion.

Associated/disassociated

When you're driving do you feel part of the car? Are you so conscious of everything you are doing and how you are driving? If so then you are associated. If on the other hand you are driving from a disassociated state then you are driving as if someone else is doing it and you yourself are watching on as if a separate person.

Whatever you are, there is no benefit of being one way over another but knowing what you are and how you process enables you to have a good understanding of yourself as a driver and be aware of how you think.

We are all different of course so it may be interesting now to think about some of your friends and the way they drive and what they drive. Can you work out what they are?

You can now apply this to other areas of your life and use this knowledge to guide you to make good decisions in your work and social life. It will also help you to understand your friends and why you get on better with some people rather than others.

CHAPTER 3

<u>HOW TO BECOME AN 'EXCELLENT'</u>
<u>DRIVER</u>

What do you want to achieve? What sort of driver do you want to be? Who would be your model of driving excellence?

In this space below write the name of your driving hero

EXERCISE

Close your eyes and imagine you are that driver and go for an imaginary drive. Choose a route that combines some high traffic situations and some open road. Give your images colour and sound like a HD film on the big screen.

Imagine you are watching yourself now as if you are watching the film of yourself.

Observe how you are driving.

Think about the beliefs you would have to drive like that.

What qualities do you observe in the driving?

List them here.

Imagine you are the passenger in that car with you driving. What qualities would they observe as a passenger?

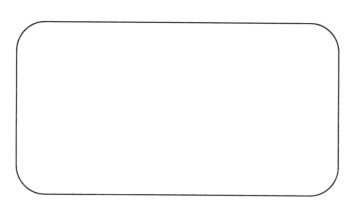

Now take a look at your lists on the previous page and score yourself out of 10 for each one in terms of your own driving. Be honest now! You don't have to show this to anyone.

Let's think about setting some goals for achieving higher scores on these qualities.

First though we need to establish your motivation for becoming a better driver and having higher scores on these qualities of driving based on your model of excellence.

What are the benefits to you of achieving this model of excellence?

First let's be internally referenced. This means asking yourself how you will feel yourself. How would it meet your own values in life? Write down below how being an excellent driver would add to your values.

Now because we are also externally referenced, some more than others, we need to ask ourselves what the benefit will be externally. How would we like others to perceive and rate our driving when we achieve the goal of excellence in driving?

Is your driving hero someone you can watch on TV or someone you have access to personally?

If they are famous they may have written a book or written in the press about their beliefs, aspirations, goals and how they work on improving. Read and observe all you can and copy what they do.

If it's someone you can drive with and talk to you can ask them about their beliefs and values, what they are thinking in different situations and you can observe how they hold the wheel, where their eyes go and how they react in different situations.

When you are modelling (this is the NLP term for copying examples of excellence) you will gain more by suspending your own analysis and judgement. Instead of assuming what the model is thinking, ask. The more aware and sensitive you can be to others, the better your driving will be.

Making assumptions is a form of distortion of the communication.

We explored your resources earlier so think now about where you have the resources you've just identified. One of your resources is also to model those examples of excellence you see around you.

When you have acquired the skill you want by modelling, it can be helpful to do this Circle of Excellence exercise.

<u>Exercise</u>

Imagine a circle drawn on the floor or if you prefer use a mat or a piece of string.

This is your circle of excellence.

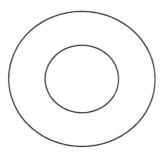

Step into it and imagine you are driving just like your model of excellence; you are that driver you admire. You are driving at your very best.

Really associate into the good images, sounds and feelings that you experience in the circle.

Now pick up your imaginary circle and place it on your steering wheel to remind yourself every time you drive.

You can use modelling and the circle of excellence for any skill you want to acquire in all parts of your life.

CHAPTER 4
<u>STATE MANAGEMENT FOR DRIVING</u>

As a young driver we can find ourselves in situations on the road when we struggle to keep calm and in control. The roads are busy and congested. Sometimes traffic can be crawling and even at a standstill. We might be in a rush to get somewhere or we're late and worried about the implications of that.

When we're stressed by the road conditions we aren't the only ones to make mistakes or poor judgements so we have to stay calm and anticipate other drivers' mistakes so we can keep safe.

There are times when we have people in the car who are distracting us, maybe singing along to the music, messing about or commenting on our driving. It can be difficult to concentrate and we find our focus not where it should be.

Our car may be playing up, making strange sounds or giving you cause for concern.

Perhaps you are driving in an unfamiliar area or conditions you are not used to such as driving rain or snow. Motorway driving takes time to master and this can be stressful, especially at night.

Maybe you are driving abroad for the first time and find the signs difficult to understand and the right of way will be different if you are driving on the other side of the road. In some countries the road conditions can be very different with windy roads, narrow roads and roads in poor condition. In some countries drivers blow their horns a lot and shout from their window, get out of the car and gesticulate a lot.

If you're driving someone else's car or a hire car or a courtesy car that is unfamiliar (especially if it is manual and you are used to an automatic) , this can be stressful too.

So there are lots of situations in which you might want to manage your emotional state.

The way we do this is to use an 'anchor'.

The metaphor of an anchor is very appropriate because when we feel adrift, lost, confused and overwhelmed by driving it is helpful to put down an anchor to stabilize ourselves and find a calm place in my mind and body.

Another reason to anchor is that we need to remind ourselves of when we are driving at our best to help us through more challenging driving situations.

The sense of calm you get from anchoring can help you find that inner resource and bring it out when and where you need it. You can anchor anywhere at any time and it takes seconds.

You may already have some <u>unconscious</u> anchors. These are anchors that remind you of feelings without you being consciously aware that they do. You can use a conscious anchor to over-ride any negative unconscious anchors.

How do we create a conscious anchor?

First we need to choose an appropriate action as an anchor. Maybe you could tap the wheel with a finger three times as your anchor?

Step 1 – Establishing the anchor

Close your eyes and think about when and where you feel calm and relaxed, strong and in control. Picture yourself there in that situation.

It does not have to be a driving situation. What can you see? Give the scene colour and clarity. Turn up the brightness and focus on everything in your picture.

What can you hear? Is there music, are people talking?

What are you doing? What is happening? Is it hot or cold, how do you feel?

When you really feel associated into the situation and as calm and confident as you could possibly be, fire the anchor. Tap three times with your finger.

Step 2 – Break state

Do something else for a moment.

Step 3 – Fire it again

Repeat step 1 and again make the images, sounds and feelings very strong before you fire the anchor.

Step 4 – Break state

Change your state for a minute – shake yourself or move about a bit.

Step 5 – Fire it again

Repeat the process. It will probably be quite quick by now.

Now you have your anchor, use it whenever you are driving and need that resource. You can establish different anchors for other resources and can use them in situations that have nothing to do with driving of course.

You will probably have occasion to drive when you are over-tired and find it hard to focus or concentrate on the road without your eyes wanting to close. This is obviously extremely dangerous.

Young men under the age of 25yrs are particularly at risk from fatigue related accidents according to research conducted by Loughborough University sleep research centre

"Sleepiness affects the brain in subtle ways, for example, producing mild euphoria and impaired judgement of risk. This "buzz" of the small hours is why casinos open at night, as punters are more likely to feel lucky, and more likely to lose. It's another reason why driving without sleep in the small hours, when our "body clock" is also at its natural nadir, is the most likely time for these crashes."

This is the type of situation where you'd establish a different anchor from the one we established for calm and control.

Now we need an anchor for being alert, awake, full of energy and aware of everything around us. So think of a time when you feel like that. It could be when playing a video game or playing a sport perhaps.

Go through exactly the same process to establish this anchor but make sure you select a different action to represent the anchor because one anchor cannot serve two different purposes.

If you had three taps for calm and control or focus then maybe squeeze your earlobe for a 'keep alert' anchor.

John Farlam suggests using NLP techniques to help you gain control of your feelings so that you can think clearly and act rationally. Here are some more ways you can use the power of your mind and imagination to conquer anger.

- See the other car as a cartoon car

- See the other driver with a big red nose, rabbit ears or anything else that looks silly or stupid

- Mentally paint the car in the same colour scheme as your bedroom when you were a kid

- Hear 'silly' music coming from the other car

- Hearing the other driver give you a grovelling apology - or just a friendly apology

- Change your own 'mental voice' to a Mickey Mouse or Donald Duck voice as you get angry

- Make up, *and believe*, a story about the other driver - Perhaps he is rushing to his dying mother's bedside, or has simply made a mistake similar to those that you sometimes make yourself (you can choose to believe anything you want to).

Although these ideas might sound silly to some people, John has used them himself and with his students when they become easily frustrated or angry with other motorists and gained great results.

The other thing about this is that if you practise responding differently it will become automatic - a useful habit that will ease some of the stress in your life.

Using simple ideas to break the cycle of frustration and anger will help prevent full blown road rage. Take a look at the exercise below and learn to relax about tailgaters.

Who's driving the car behind?

You might look in the mirror and feel uncomfortable about the driver behind. Maybe the driver is obviously angry or maybe you are simply misreading the 'signs' - either way the feelings are the same...

For example, is the lady in the image on the next page frustrated with you or giving way with a friendly gesture? Whatever her intention, if you feel that her gesture and expression is hostile it will have a negative effect on the way you feel, this could be anger or frustration - or maybe you feel bad about getting in the way...

Try this!

By changing your mental image of the person behind you will also change how you feel... It doesn't matter how you do it – You can picture a clown behind, or that the car behind is a bright pink Barbie Car. By thinking differently about the 'idiots' on the road, angry or upset drivers can gain the capability of controlling their feelings

It is difficult, if not impossible, to hold two conflicting ideas at once.

When we are thinking of the other driver in a humorous way, the humour will usually diffuse feelings of anger leaving us in a more useful state - free to make a more rational choice about our response. A person who 'can't stand idiots on the road' will have nothing to be mad about when given a mental choice of humour - safe drivers don't get mad.

The NLP principle underlying the above is, 'If you keep doing what you've always done, you'll keep getting what you've always got' - if you have a tendency to get annoyed with other drivers, doing what you've always done will result in reduced in safety - the way you feel will influence the way you drive. Thinking differently enables a more useful and safer response.

Fear is the body's response to something you associate with pain. It's like an unconscious negative anchor as discussed in the previous chapter. Without thinking or being aware you have anchored this thing to fear. Therefore what we need to do is break the anchor and therefore the negative associations. The process is called for obvious reasons perhaps, 'disassociation'.

EXERCISE

Find a quiet place and use your newly created anchor for being relaxed and calm, confident and able to cope with anything.

Now imagine that you are in a cinema, perhaps your favourite local one. Picture the interior and visualise yourself sitting there with the screen in front of you and people around you.

On the screen in front of you there is a movie of you in the situation you fear. It's a horror movie.

As you watch the movie of yourself doing the thing you fear, imagine you can now move to the projection box and switch the film to black and white, you can take away the sound and make it silent or add a sound track of your own choosing. You could make the film a comedy or a feature film using your favourite actors. Turn the film into a more enjoyable one for you.

Now start the movie again in its new form from the projection booth. See yourself in the cinema, in the audience, watching it. Yes you are watching yourself watching the new film.

When the movie is finished, rewind it scene by scene. When you've done that, repeat it again going backwards only do it faster.

This constant repetition of rewinding the film in a disassaciated state, watching yourself in it, enables you to effectively change the experience into something that you no longer find fearful.

Another way to conquer fear is to work out what the trigger is for your fear. We do this by first ackowledging whether you are visual, auditory or kinaesthetic as a driver.

Now think about the structure of what you fear.

By this I mean, what happens first, second, third? What is the trigger for your fear. Is it something you see, something you hear or something you feel?

What we are going to do is SWISH the negative trigger into something positive in a similar way to what we did in the cinema example.

1) Write down what happens just <u>before</u> you feel fear.

The trigger for me is.............................

Then what happens? Write it down here.

2) Make a picture in your head of what happens when you get that trigger and imagine it like a picture on the

screen as if it's a movie at the cinema.

3) Now think of what you would <u>like</u> to happen instead next time that trigger goes off in your head. Write it down in the box below.

4) Make a picture in your head of this now. Then place that picture in the bottom left hand corner of the screen with your bad image in it. Like this.

5) Now say out loud 'SWISH' and make the good image in the corner switch with the bad image in the middle.

You will need to practice it a few times and when you have it perfect you can use it every time you see, hear or feel that trigger in your head.

Lots of drivers have a fear of the unknown. They fear getting lost or driving at night.

Driving at night has the additional aspect of tiredness and having to allow for other people's possible drink driving. Fog, frost and ice are also more likely at this time.

Apart from the obvious practical things you can do like keeping the windscreen clean and driving slower you can use your circle of excellence to remind yourself how you drive when you are driving your best, like your model of excellence. You can use the SWISH to choose a positive reaction to the driving conditions such as relishing the challenge to prove what a good driver you are. You can use your anchoring to anchor a calm state.

Perhaps you feel fearful when you are driving close to very large trucks? You could SWISH them into something less scary.

All these NLP techniques need to be practised again and again so that they become second nature. You will find as you familiarise yourself with them in your driving that not only will your driving become much better but also you will be using them in your everyday work and social life.

References

John Farlam www.smartdriving.co.uk

Don Palmer www.donpalmer.co.uk

Superdriver   John Whitmore   Motorbooks Int.

Lightning Source UK Ltd.
Milton Keynes UK
UKOW05f1331211116
288165UK00019B/1195/P